The Soul of an Artist

The Spiritual and Motivational Power of Music

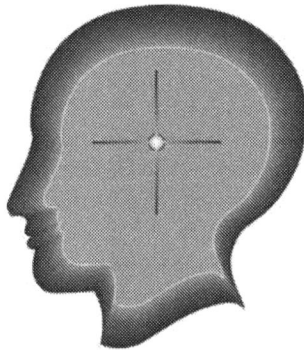

By O. Bernard Smalls

THE SOUL OF AN ARTIST
The Spiritual and Motivational Power of Music

ISBN Number: 978-0-6151-5409-1
Printed in the United States of America
Published by: O. Bernard Smalls
Copyright 2007 by O. Bernard Smalls Companies

Introduction

I am an artist, a musician and, most of all, a communicator. Some people call me a space cowboy! Others call me a motivational speaker. To stay true to my labels, I want to use this book to stimulate and motivate you. The purpose of this book is simple. Its purpose is to bring people to the understanding of the motivational energy and power of music. Music is a powerful tool that can be used to bring about positive social change. I invite you to read, reflect and enjoy. There are no chapters to this book. You can start or stop on any page and reflect on the concept or quote. I hope that this simple treatise will awaken the *artist* within you.

Bernard Smalls
Suwanee – Atlanta, Georgia

"Our deepest fear is not that we are inadequate. Our deepest fear is that we are powerful beyond measure. It is our light, not our darkness, that most frightens us. We ask ourselves, who am I to be brilliant, gorgeous, talented, fabulous? Actually, who are you NOT to be? You are a child of God. Your playing small does not serve the world. There is nothing enlightened about shrinking so that other people won't feel insecure around you. We were born to make manifest the glory of God that is within us. It is not just in some of us, it is in everyone. And as we let our own light shine, we unconsciously give other people permission to do the same. As we are liberated from our own fear, our presence automatically liberates others."

~ Marianne Williamson

THE
MOTIVATIONAL
POWER OF
Music

Hey music lover!

Relax, get your favorite beverage and let's TAP-IN TO THE SPIRITUAL AND MOTIVATIONAL POWER OF MUSIC!

I want to start out with some powerful scientific facts about the energizing power of the art we love so much. We will share from much research that I and others have done that reveals powerful concepts about the power of music. I want to show you that music is some serious stuff! Music has spiritual and motivational power.

Music's EFFECT

In 1974, Fabien Maman was working as a professional jazz musician. He noticed that certain musical keys had an energizing effect on both the musicians and the audience.

Fabien worked with the French physicist Joel Sternheimer. Sternheimer had discovered that elementary particles vibrate at frequencies in accordance with musical laws.

A few years later, Fabien met a senior researcher at the National Center for Scientific Research in Paris. They devoted a year-and-a-half to study the effects of sound on normal and malignant cells. Using drums, gongs, flutes, guitar, bass and a xylophone, they investigated the effects of sound on healthy blood cells, hemo-globin, and the `Hela' cancer cell from the uterus. They found that even at 30-40 decibels, the sound always produced noticeable changes in the cells. As the sounds progressed up the musical scale there would be an `explosion' of the cancer cells at a certain frequency as the sound traveled outward from the centre of the cell to its outer membrane.

That is powerful stuff! Realize that your music has tremendous effect!

"For a musician to be the best he must unite with God."

—Bernard Smalls

Voice ~

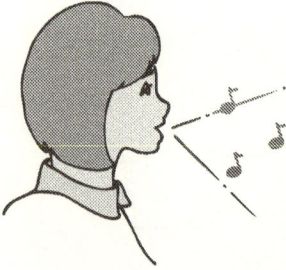

The experiment yielded the most dramatic results when the human voice was used. Fabien says, `Near the end of the scale, usually around the seventh interval, the cancer cells exploded. It appears that the cancer cells were not able to support a progressive accumulation of frequencies.' 'The healthy cells appeared supple and able to freely receive, absorb and return the energy. In contrast, the cancer cells appeared inflexible and immutable in their structure.'

In experimental sessions on actual cancer patients, the music produced equally astonishing results. I believe that this is because music is positive spiritual power. Cancer is a negative destructive force.

Female volunteers with breast cancer were taught to tone the whole scale, using a violin to keep a base note for 2 minutes at a time. They spent three and one-half hours a day doing this for a month. One woman's tumor disappeared completely. If you doubt this, remember that David's music healed King Saul!

WOW
(wonder of wonders)

music has

supernatural

power!

MUSIC???

Music helped develop civilization

   We pray to it,

      Dance to it,

      Sing and have fun to it,

We pass the day,

   Drive the car,

      Wash the windows,

Sip some of our favorite beverage,

   We eat our meals,

Wash our clothes

   and bury our dead with it.

I LUV MUSIC!

> *"Music is the electrical soil in which the spirit lives, thinks, and invents."*
>
> –Ludwig van Beethoven

Many artists see music as a luxury, just as a fun thing. I have come to understand that music has tremendous motivational and spiritual power. Music is absolutely necessary to help humans reach their full potential.

As Beethoven said: *music is the electrical soil in which the spirit, lives, thinks and invents.* Music has the motivational ability to awaken the spirit in man and help to release our creativity.

"Music is good for us, physically, emotionally and spiritually."

–Anonymous

MUSICOLOGY!

Have you ever thought about why we love music so much? Is it just because it sounds good?

We are surrounded by sounds at all times. The art that derives from our sense of hearing is music.

Music is order given to sound.

Music has many different functions. It has been and remains a major element in nearly all religious rituals.

"Music makes us more inventive!"

"Has anyone ever observed that music emancipates the spirit? Gives wings to thought? And that the more one becomes a musician the more one is a philosopher?"

–Friedrich Nietzche

I have personally met several musicians who were deep philosophers. They would stay up all night talking about philosophies of life, religion and so forth—some were so deep they went off the deep end. Many of these musicians would often discuss social and political issues as they inhaled that stuff. You know what I am talking about J.

Music has social power. Bob Marley proved that by impacting the whole nation of Jamaica with his strong social message in his music. No society present or past has ever lacked music. Music is one of the few human universals which put us all on the same level such as food and sex!

Man has used music to go war and retailers have used music to create a mood for shoppers to spend money... and the beat goes on...

YOUR INSTRUMENT BECOMES AN EXTENSION OF YOU!

Does music really have inherent power that we have neglected?

Remember, when David played, Saul was healed....

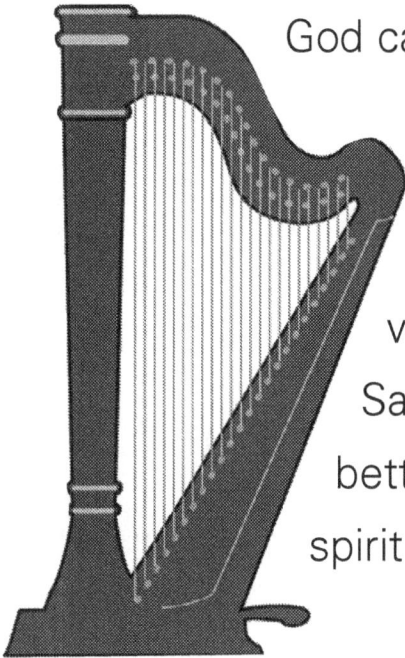

Whenever the spirit from God came upon Saul, David would take his harp and play. Then relief would come to Saul; he would feel better, and the evil spirit would leave him.

1 Samuel 16:23

Music Has Extraordinary Results

Even in the natural world hearing good music has awesome potential to help us.

Here are some natural facts that illustrate how music can produce extraordinary results in people:

♫ Gerard Depardieu, the great French actor could hardly string a sentence together before he embarked on a course of sound therapy.

♫ Ronald Parkinson PhD, a music professor at Northern Illinois University keeps his Parkinson's disease at bay by playing the harp.

♫ Students who sing or play a musical instrument at school score higher in all other subjects than other non-musical students.

David was a skilled and
gifted musician…

He was a King, a Poet,
and a Prophet & last
but not least, a MUSICIAN!

- He was referred to as Israel's versatile King.

- He was considered least likely to succeed…

- He was cunning!

Cunning Defined:
the Hebrew word for
cunning means skill,
expertise, creativity,
dexterity, ingenuity, ability...

player on the harp...
            he shall play...

"Play always as if
a master was listening."

–Robert Schumann

DAVID!!!

MUSIC'S HEALING POWER!

The Bible says that David played and King Saul was refreshed . . . and the evil spirit departed from him. **Now that's what I call supernatural music therapy!**

Music had a place of high priority in the life of David because David was a man after God's heart. Music is a high priority in the heart of God. Music was even used in the transferring of the Ark of the Covenant by King David.

1 Samuel 16: 17:
provide me a man that can play well...

HEY ARTIST!
YOU HAVE
CRE8TIVE
ABILITY

I preach with

creative,

artistic ability.

How? I play!

I bring good Newz,

I preach peace.

Music is my

apostolic tool.

–Bernard Smalls

David's playing brought peace
to Saul...

*"If the king
loves music,
there is little
wrong in the
land."*

–Mencius

MUSIC = HEALING POWER

It is a known fact that illnesses have often responded to sound and music.

Research reveals conclusive evidence that music can be used to reduce high blood pressure and anxiety. Music can break up cancer cells in our bodies and can help to heal mental illnesses.

Scientists concluded that preferred music may produce a positive emotional experience that can release hormones, which create a healing effect in the body.

The director of Baltimore hospital's coronary care unit says that half an hour of classical music produces the same effect as ten milligrams of valium.

♫ ♫ ♫

"Music washes away from the soul the everyday dust of life."

–Berthold Auerbach

"First was the world as
one great Cymbal
Where Jarring Windes to
infant Nature plaid.

All Musick was a solitary
sound, the hollow Rocks and
murm'ring Fountains bound.

Then Musick, the Mosaique
of the Air, Did of all these a
solemn noise prepare With
which She gain'd the Empire
of the Ear, Including all
between Earth and Sphear."

—Andrew Marvell

Using Your Brain Power

I have always found the study of the brain to be fascinating. Most studies reveal that we use very little of the brain's capacity. It's like we have been given this terrific technology, but few have studied the owner's manual of how to run the brain.

Recent studies have revealed what we know as left brain/right brain; i.e. the brain has two basic hemispheres, the left hemisphere and the right hemisphere. The left is the arena of logic, while the right is the arena of creativity.

Another exciting topic related to more effective brain function is *"the ultradian cycle."* This is a concept about the left and right hemispheres of the brain. This cycle relates to how the brain flows between hemispheres as one goes through daily activities.

When you flow into the right hemisphere you move into imagination, ideas, vision and other such creative concepts. To stay centered and whole as a person, you need both hemispheres of the brain to function properly. Flowing from left-brain to right brain is a key to relaxing.

A relaxed body = an alert mind.

When you are in the relaxed state your brain has the tendency to sprout new concepts. When you're sprouting, just sprout! Learn to flow, relax, and enjoy sprouting. Sprouting is the result of seeds being planted in the brain in the form of ideas, music, art, literature and many other creative forms of communication.

Relaxed body = alert mind, which births innovation, creativity, and ideas.

Creative people tend to be more right-brained because artistic creativity is a function of the right hemisphere of the brain!

People who are left-brain dominant tend to be:

- organized
- logical
- detail oriented
- practical
- analytical

People who are right-brain dominant tend to be:

- cluttered
- emotion-based
- free thinking
- intuitive
- deep thinkers

http://continuingeducation.suite101.com/article.cfm/leftbrainrightbrain

We must learn to MASTER our brains.

Master is an acronym meaning:

Mind

Acquire

Search-out

Trigger memory

Exhibit what we know

Reflect on process

It's great to have more insight on how to run the human brain.

I think the concept of Mind Mapping is awesome and that it could change the way artists function and release more creativity!

MOZART

Research reveals that the music of Mozart assists both sides of the brain to work together overcoming the left brain dominance of our Western society. Scientists suggest that listening to music can help to improve concentration and enhance our ability to make intuitive leaps.

The most in-depth use of music to accelerate learning was developed by the Bulgarian psychologist, Geogi Lozanov. Developed initially for adults studying foreign languages, his technique known as `Suggestopedia' has been incorporated into curricula throughout Europe and the United States. He has proved that slow creative music such as jazz or classical music improves learning.

Before you can share your music with others you must reach inside— in solitude – meditation..."

–Anonymous

My Musical Journey
GIVE THE DRUMMER SUM!!!

"The drummer is an inspirer, a leader and a prophet. The blow of the drumstick translates itself not merely into sound, but into spiritual reverberation..."

–Anonymous

Uh....good God, give the drummer some! R.I.P. JB? James Brown was definitely an influence on my early music career. I grew up on his stuff.

Music has been an important part of my life as far back as I can remember. I have come to believe that it is my Divine destiny to play.

I can still remember that as a kid in elementary school, the teacher had to often command me to quit drumming on the desk and to stop thumping on everything.

"When drums speak out, laws hold their tongues."

–Thomas Fuller

Drumming for local bands continued all through high school (including two of the best rhythm and blues and funk bands in Charleston, South Carolina in the early 70s.) I was growing up fast and was often being slipped into the back door of clubs since I was under-aged for being in an environment where alcohol was being sold.

THE OAKLAND STROKE!

During my senior year in high school our band hooked up with an agent in Oakland, California and we were invited to move to the Bay area. I thought this is a dream come true. Right out of high school I can hit the road and go to the Bay area of all places. YES!

So there I was, three months out of high school on the road to the Oakland-San Fran Bay area (where Sly Stone and Tower of Power, two my musical idols were) to pursue my dream.

In Oakland, we immediately found out that our agent had tremendous power and influence in the Bay Area. He was the man! We also found out that music was not the only business he was in. He was also in the oldest profession known to man – "prostitution." He was a bona-fide "pimp."

THE DOWNSTROKE!

During our time in Oakland our band struck a potential deal with Motown. While living in this fantasy we learned a powerful lesson that I later found was Biblical. That lesson is simply this: Pride leads to a fall! Most musicians have no shortage of pride.

While we were smoking that stuff, getting drunk, spending nights with Mr. K's (the pimp/promoter) girls and bragging about how much money we were going to make, the whole deal with MOTOWN fell through! Pride was the down-stroke...

It was due to an enormous power struggle at the top between two of the key players about who was the greatest. Talk about pride! Our band leader who was very talented (that guy could flat sing) was lifted up with pride about his talent being our ticket to success. Mr. K's agency was fed up with it especially since our band leader had started to challenge Mr. K. and say I don't need you or your money.

The agency eventually sent us on tour to Anchorage, Alaska and dropped us like a hot potato! My advice to artists: keep your ego in check! Pride goes before a fall!

"Ever since their invention drums have been used in rituals. The practice of using the drum as an altar has been carried into modern times, with soldiers in the field using an upturned drum as the focus of acts of worship!"

"I recognize greed; I know when a man is playing for money!"

–Coleman Hawkins

MUSIC AND LEARNING

We have all heard the saying "knowledge is power!" Many have not understood that music has tremendous potential as a learning tool.

We must understand this if we are ever going to see how important it is for us to properly use the gift of music.

Many musicians just see music as a fun, cool thing that they love to do. They just love to "groove" as it were. Even though the groove is good, it is important to understand the spiritual and motivational implications involved.

SOUL POWER

"But now bring me a minstrel (musician). And when it came to pass that the minstrel (musician) played, that the hand of the LORD came upon him."

—II Kings 3: 15

The phrase "Soul Power" was made popular in the late 60s and early 70s. It was directly related to the belief system of the African-American during the civil rights movement. James Brown even sang: *"you know we need it soul power…gotta have it soul power."*

You are a spirit, you have a soul and you live in a body. The soul is the mind, the will and the emotions, so there is such a thing as soul power.

Here is a great question:

Why has so much
SOUL MUSIC
had its foundation
in the Church?

James Brown, Aretha Franklin, Stevie Wonder, Little Richard and even Elvis started out in what we call "gospel music." I believe that the Church was where they first felt the spiritual power of music.

As a drummer who has played professionally for a living, I can tell you first-hand what I first felt in Church! My dad and granddad were Methodist ministers in the "black church"...man you talk about rhythm.

> *Real music is not for wealth,*
> *not for honors, joys of the mind,*
> *but a path*
> *for realization and salvation.*
>
> –ALI AKABAR RHAN

I can still remember most of the rhythms and hand-clapping sequences when the "spirit" came in on Sunday mornings (or afternoon). Man, they tore it up!

As a kid you could look into the faces of the adults and see that they were feeling the power of something.

"*Music* is one of the greatest gifts that God has given us: it is divine: and therefore Satan is the enemy. For with its aid many dire temptations are overcome; the devil does not stay where music is."

–Martin Luther

By the way, they had no drums in Promise Land United Methodist Church (drums were too worldly) they used their hand to clap it up or down. My dad bought us the first drum-set from Reliable Pawn Shop for a grand total of $119.00 (that was a lot of money back in the day).

 I have felt the power when the band got into what I call the groove and it seemed that we could do no wrong. We were tapping into the spiritual power of music. Music is good! I love music! Music is a tremendous spiritual force.

I have played at record-hops (along with records while people danced, in bands with just a rhythm section), in bands with horn sections, in jazz combos, in rock bands, funk bands and even in country and western bands. My motto was *will play for fun and food*. You could say "I have felt first-handedly the soul power of music."

Even the Bible confirms the spiritual power of music. A Prophet of old, when needing help to get him into the flow, said to his helper "bring me a musician."

Why? Because when the musician played the hand (power) of the LORD came upon him. Yes music has awesome spiritual power which you too can tap into for good.

Music esp. cymbals were used at the dedication of the Ark...

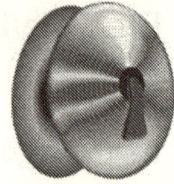

The Bible says that in the mouth of two or three witnesses every word should be established. Here are several words or scriptures that prove that God has put a high priority on music. Think and meditate on these. **Selah!**

1. **1 Samuel 16:23**

   Whenever the spirit from God came upon Saul, **David** would take his **harp** and play. Then relief would come to Saul; he would feel better, and the evil spirit would leave him.
   1 Samuel 16:22-23 (in Context)
   1 Samuel 16 (Whole Chapter)

2. **1 Samuel 18:10**

   The next day an evil spirit from God came forcefully upon Saul. He was prophesying in his house, while **David** was playing the **harp**, as he usually did. Saul had a spear in his hand
   1 Samuel 18:9-11 (in Context)
   1 Samuel 18 (Whole Chapter)

3. **2 Samuel 6:5**

   David and the whole house of Israel were celebrating with all their might before the LORD, with songs and with **harps**, lyres, tambourines, sistrums and cymbals.
   2 Samuel 6:4-6 (in Context)
   2 Samuel 6 (Whole Chapter)

4. **1 Chronicles 13:8**

   David and all the Israelites were celebrating with all their might before God, with songs and with **harps**, lyres, tambourines, cymbals and trumpets.
   1 Chronicles 13:7-9 (in Context)
   1 Chronicles 13 (Whole Chapter)

5. **1 Chronicles 15:16**

   David told the leaders of the Levites to appoint their brothers as singers to sing joyful songs, accompanied by musical instruments: lyres, **harps** and cymbals.
   1 Chronicles 15:15-17 (in Context)
   1 Chronicles 15 (Whole Chapter)

6. **1 Chronicles 25:1**

   [*The Singers*] **David**, together with the commanders of the army, set apart some of the sons of Asaph, Heman and Jeduthun for the ministry of prophesying, accompanied by **harps**, lyres and cymbals. Here is the list of the men who performed this service:

   1 Chronicles 25:1-3 (in Context)
   1 Chronicles 25 (Whole Chapter)

7. **2 Chronicles 29:25**

   He stationed the Levites in the temple of the LORD with cymbals, **harps** and lyres in the way prescribed by **David** and Gad the king's seer and Nathan the prophet; this was commanded by the LORD through his prophets.

   2 Chronicles 29:24-26 (in Context)
   2 Chronicles 29 (Whole Chapter)

8. **Amos 6:5**

   You strum away on your **harps** like **David** and improvise on musical instruments.

   Amos 6:4-6 (in Context)
   Amos 6 (Whole Chapter)

Scientific Proof!

For those of you who struggle with believing the Bible, here are some areas of scientific proof that music has tremendous power to produce good results in humanity.

AUTISM

The parents of autistic children have found that music therapy can help their children to interact with them in a normal way. Sam, a seven-year-old child diagnosed with autism at the age of two was unable to tolerate any loud sound. He had tantrums and when his mother sang to him he would say to her, "stop singing." After sound therapy he said to his mother "Hold me. Hum with me."

BABIES

The *Journal of the American Medical Association* reported in that in a study of expectant mothers, many who listened to music during childbirth did not require an anesthetic. Listening to music releases endorphins, and this decreases the need for medication. It also provides a distraction from pain and relieves anxiety.

In another study of pregnant mothers, babies were found to prefer Mozart and Vivaldi to other composers in early, as well as the later stages, of pregnancy. When mothers listened to rock music, fetuses would kick violently and have increased heart rates. The energy of the music affected the soul and spirit of the unborn baby.

PHYSIOLOGICAL EFFECTS

Researches at the John Hopkins University have found that rock music causes people to eat faster and to eat a larger volume of food, while slow classical music makes people eat more slowly and consume less. Are you in a hurry? Need to move faster? Put on some rock music. We all know that when working out, loud energetic music communicates energy to our souls and bodies.

Finally, David often said "Bless the LORD O my soul..." So God loves soul music. WOW!

MUSIC & WARFARE

I spent years as a student of Theology pursuing spiritual knowledge. I find it an extremely interesting topic. Theology literally means the study of God.

One story that has always amazed me being a musician is when the nation of Israel was instructed by God to put the musicians and singers before the Army in a major military engagement.

MUSIC WINS THE BATTLE!

22 As they began to sing and praise, the LORD set ambushes against the men of Ammon and Moab and Mount Seir who were invading Judah, and they were defeated.

23 The men of Ammon and Moab rose up against the men from Mount Seir to destroy and annihilate them. After they finished slaughtering the men from Seir, they helped to destroy one another.
2 Chronicles 20: 22-23

Just think for a moment of the awesome power in music displayed in this true account. What audacity it took to send the musicians and singers into a fierce battle before the army. God used music to win the battle!

"Music praises God. Music is well or better able to praise him than the building of the church and all its decoration; it is the churches greatest ornament"

–Igor Stravinsky

Music can be used as a weapon of war because it contains spiritual (invisible) power.

> ## "Every place we play is church."
> –Paul Lesh

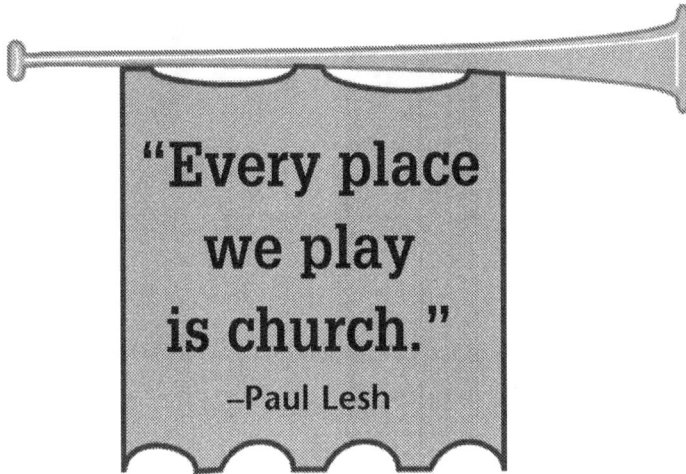

Yes! There is tremendous spiritual power in music. I like to refer to this as warfare music. Many wars have been won by the inspiration of the music that ignited the army to fight to the finish.

Warfare music brings on the spirit of battle and gives tremendous breakthroughs in realms far beyond human intellect.

For instance, in history, drums are often used when African tribes are about to attack.

THE POWER OF SOUND!

It is extremely important that we understand the power of sound in general or what is musically called **RESONANCE**.

To gain a simple insight into the breakthrough power of sound, we must understand the word resonance. Resonance means; timbre, reverberation or simply sound. Let me illustrate: When an opera singer vibrates a glass with their voice, they have matched the resonant frequency of the glass.

As the singer increases the volume of their sound, the resonance becomes too great for the forces that hold the glass together and it shatters!

This reveals that a greater power dominates a lesser power. Spiritual (invisible) forces are generally more powerful than natural forces. Music is an invisible spiritual force.

David and the whole house of Israel were celebrating with all their might before the LORD, with songs and with **harps**, lyres, tambourines, sistrums and cymbals.

SOUND HEALING

There is an ancient Greek saying, 'Men have song as a physician for pain.'

An illustration of the invisible power of music is obvious in how modern medicine now uses sound waves to break up kidney stones and gallstones. Every organ, every bone, every cell in the body has its own resonant frequency.

Through the power of sound healing it may be possible to bring the diseased organ into harmony with the rest of the body, hence avoiding the need for drugs or surgery, such as with kidney or gallstones.

Sound has been used as a healing force for thousands of years. All ancient civilizations used sound for healing.

Traditional cultures still surviving today understand the remarkable healing power that lies in sound. The results of sound on blood, water, cancer cells and a range of conditions are astonishing.

Here are some historical, empirical examples of the power of sound:

♫ Egyptian papyri over 2,600 years old refer to incantations as cures for infertility and rheumatic pain.

♫ The ancient Greeks believed music had the power to heal body and soul. They used the flute and the lyre for treating illnesses such as gout and sciatica.

♫ It is reported that Alexander the Great's sanity was restored by music played on the lyre.

Sound healing is the therapeutic application of sound frequencies to the body/mind of a person with the intention of bringing them into a state of harmony and health.

The dictionary defines 'harmony' as 'congruity of parts to their whole or to one another.' 'Health' is defined as 'the state of being bodily and mentally vigorous and free of disease.'

The French ear, nose and throat specialist,
Dr. Alfred Tomatis has devoted the last 50
years to understanding the ear and its
function. He believes that the ear is the
most important of all our sense organs. The
ear controls the body's sense of balance,
rhythm and movement and is the conductor
of the entire nervous system. Through the
medulla, the auditory nerve connects with all
the muscles of the body. Hence, muscle tone,
equilibrium, flexibility and vision are affected
by sound.

GOOD VIBRATION!

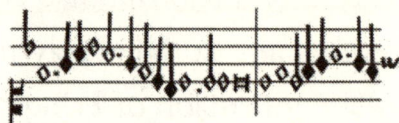

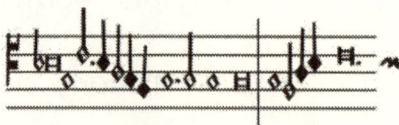

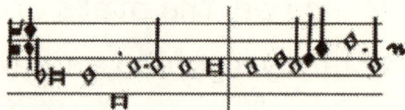

In the 1960s, Hans Jenny, a Swiss scientist, spent over ten years conducting experiments to discover the effects of sound waves on materials placed on metal plates vibrated with sound. Jenny came to the conclusion that sound creates form and that the entire human body had its own sound made up of all the sounds of its cells, tissues and organs.

Scientific Research into Sound

In the 18th century Ernest Chladni, a German physicist, found that when a violin bow was drawn vertically across the rim of a metal plate the sound waves produced created patterns in sand sprinkled on the plate. Different musical tones would cause the sand particles to move into geometric patterns.

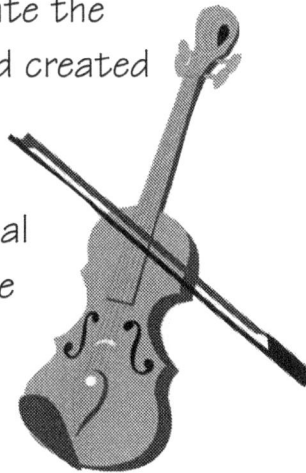

SPIRIT BEINGS

Man is a being created in the likeness and image of God. What is God like? God is a spirit. Man is a spirit being, he has a soul and he lives in a physical body.

God is a Spirit and they that worship Him must worship in spirit...
John 4: 24

Music is a spiritual force that originated in the heart of God.

According to the Bible God had a master-musician named Lucifer who apparently was the worship leader in heaven. He was fabulous! Because of his beauty and talent he got the "big head" and decided that he would take over God's job. Well he was wrong and was cast down from heaven to earth.

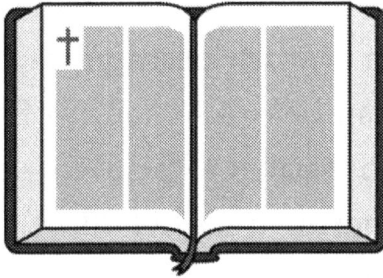

I am persuaded that his rebellion is the reason for the destructive spiritual power in the music of the world today.

Yes, music has spiritual power that can be good or evil because music is a spiritual force.

Satan
& Music

The **big question** is:

"Was Satan in charge of music in Heaven?"

Here is my answer:

Ezekiel 28:13 of the KJV and NKJV seem to hint that Satan was involved with music in Heaven. The two Scripture passages that describe Satan before he fell are Ezekiel 28:12-19 and Isaiah 14:12-15. Satan was the "anointed cherub" (Ezekiel 28:14). He was adorned with every precious jewel imaginable (Ezekiel 28:13). He was "the model of perfection, full of wisdom and perfect in beauty" (Ezekiel 28:12b).

Likely he was the highest of all angels. He was persuasive enough to convince one-third of the angels to join him in his rebellion (Revelation 12:4). Even after his fall from heaven, not even Michael the archangel dares to stand up to him without the Lord's help (Jude 9). Satan fell because of pride. It is amazing to watch the pride in the musicians of the world today. Humility seems to be a rare bird among musical artists.

Satan did not like being "second best" (sound like some of the cats I have met in jam sessions) . He wanted to be God: "You said in your heart, 'I will ascend to heaven; I will raise my throne above the stars of God; I will sit enthroned on the mount of assembly, on the utmost heights of the sacred mountain'" (Isaiah 14:13).

Was Satan the head musician? Considering the fact that the angels constantly worship God (Isaiah 6:3; Revelation 4:8), it is possible that Satan led in worship.

13 Thou hast been in Eden the garden of God; every precious stone was thy covering, the sardius, topaz, and the diamond, the beryl, the onyx, and the

jasper, the sapphire, the emerald, and the carbuncle, and gold: <u>the workmanship of thy tabrets and of thy pipes</u> was prepared in thee in the day that thou wast created. Ezekiel 28: 13

"Was Satan in charge of music in Heaven?"

Tabrets and pipes are musical terms. Selah! (Think about these things…)

"I am persuaded that some Christian artists "cross over" into the mainstream. As John Wesley said, 'the world is my Parish!'"

—Bernard Smalls

MUSIC &
NUMBERS

Pythagoras of Samos (Greek 582 BC, circa 507 BC) was a Greek mathematician, astronomer, scientist and philosopher, founder of the mathematical, mystic, religious, and scientific society called Pythagoreans. He is best known as "the father of numbers," Pythagoras made influential contributions to philosophy and religious teaching in the late 6th century BC. Because legend and obscurity cloud his work, even more than with the other pre-Socratics, one can say little with confidence about his life and teachings. We do know that Pythagoras and his students believed that everything was related to mathematics and that numbers were the ultimate reality and, through mathematics, everything could be predicted and measured in rhythmic patterns or cycles. Pythagoras once said that "number is the ruler of forms and ideas."

> *One good thing about music,*
> *when it hits, you feel no pain.*
>
> –Bob Marley

Pythagoras observed that when the blacksmith struck his anvil, different notes were produced according to the weight of the hammer. Number (in this case "amount of weight") seemed to govern musical tone. When a piano player strikes a key, the hammer strikes the strings and the amount of force with which she strikes the key and the length of the chord determines the resulting sound. In reality this is all mathematical. Further, he observed that if you take two strings in the same degree of tension, and then divide one of them exactly in half, when they are plucked, the pitch of the shorter string is exactly one octave higher than the longer: Pythagoreans are credited for having brought measure to music through the study of the monochord, pipes, and bells.

Pythagoras: From Wikipedia, the free encyclopedia

Some people say that God is not interested in numbers. I disagree because he wrote a book called Numbers – DUH! Numbers are an important part of music.

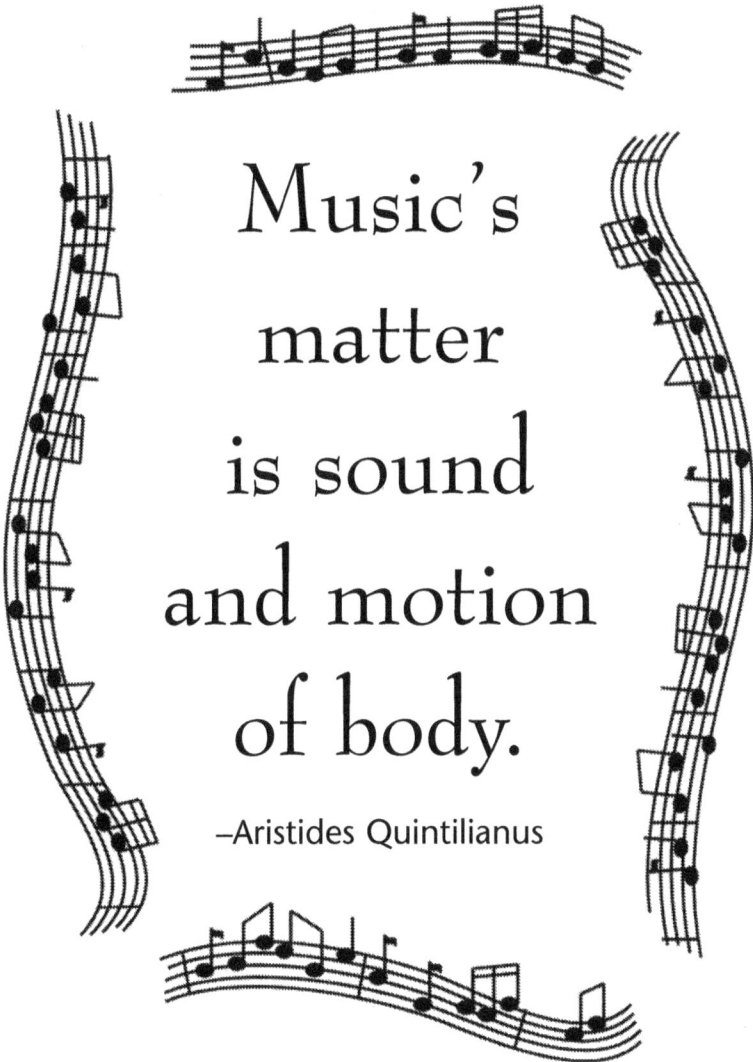

Music's matter is sound and motion of body.

–Aristides Quintilianus

MUSIC AS MEDICINE

Don Campbell, in his book *The Mozart Effect*, shows how music, particularly Mozart's, has all kinds of beneficial effects for human health. Scientists suggest that listening to Mozart helps us to improve our powers of concentration and enhances our ability to make intuitive leaps, by organizing the firing pattern of neurons in the cerebral cortex. The fetus tends to prefer Mozart and Vivaldi to other composers. When pregnant mothers listened to Mozart and Vivaldi, the babies' heart rates invariably steadied and kicking declined. Slower tempo music slows our breathing rate. The human heartbeat will tend to match the rhythm of music.

Listening to Pacabel's Cannon, for instance, at around 64 beats per minute, the rate of a resting heart beat, will slow our breathing rate and heart rate and change our brain wave pattern from beta to alpha. Music will also calm our nervous system and affect metabolism.

The pitch and rhythm of music influence the limbic system, affecting our emotions. Scientists concluded that preferred music "may elicit a profound positive emotional experience that can trigger the release of hormones, which can contribute to a lessening of those factors which enhance the disease process."

Music is now used to reduce the pain and anxiety of patients undergoing dental treatment and surgical operations. In a study of 59,000 patients, 97% of patients stated that music really helped them to relax in the post-operative situation and during surgery with regional anesthesia.

In his research, Dr Mike Lewis found that classical music works on the whole brain, whereas pop music affects only one side of the brain. He says, 'I recommend that those who are looking for a peak experience try classical. Mozart is a great place to start, but it is a question of trial and error, find what works for you.'

Dancing is a social response to the power of the groove!

–Bernard Smalls

THE POWER OF
singing

Why sing? Singing can be extremely therapeutic. For thousands of years people have sung as part of their daily life. We are the first generation of people who have machines to sing for us.

We can combat the invasion of external noise by singing, humming or toning. By using our voice we can tune ourselves up. With a little bit of help, most people can sing in tune.

Those who think they can't sing generally have frequencies missing from their hearing. Once these missing frequencies are restored, people are often amazed that they can sing in tune.

Sing unto the LORD a new song...

Psalm 33: 3a

People who sing regularly generally enjoy better health than the rest of the population. As a student of theology, I realize how important it is for each of us to use our own voice to keep ourselves healthy.

Of all the professions, orchestral conductors enjoy the longest life span and often continue to work into their eighties.

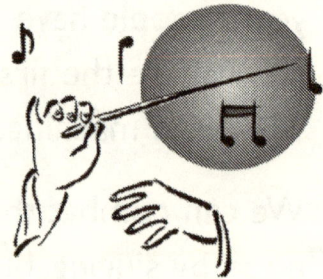

Music is a spiritual doorway – its power comes from the fact it plugs directly to the soul!

–Peter Gabriel

SINGING & TONING

Dr Tomatis found that a child traumatized by an enraged or screaming adult learns to survive by shutting out these noises. Once the hearing shuts down, the child will find it hard to learn.

This explains why some people can sing in tune while others consider themselves 'tone deaf.' It is impossible for us to make a sound unless we have heard that sound or note before. I have found from experience in teaching voice work that once a person's hearing is reawakened, then they can begin to hear what is sung to them and can then accurately copy this sound.

Toning is defined as 'to make sound with an elongated vowel for an extended period.' Toning with other people creates a feeling of unity, and this is why corporate praise and worship in unity is good and pleasant. It also helps us to release stress and repressed emotions. Regular toning and humming helps to re-energize the body and restore health to the mind, body and spirit.

Toning has a neurochemical effect on the body, boosting the immune system and causing the release of endorphins. Toning assists in good breathing and posture. The muscles of the digestive system are massaged and stimulated by regular toning. Toning has also been effective in relieving insomnia.

Alfred Wolfson was a German-born singing teacher who was plagued by the sounds of artillery and human agony that he experienced as a soldier in the trenches in World War I. Wolfson cured himself of aural hallucinations by singing the terrible sounds that haunted him. He went on to develop a therapeutic method that was based on using the voice. Using Jung's concept of the anima and animus, Wolfson taught that by extending the vocal range through singing exercises, one could contact the opposite polarity within oneself, thereby integrating the psyche and healing a variety of psychological and physical conditions.

Laurel Elizabeth Keys, in her book *Toning the Creative Power of the Voice*, says, "A whiny weak voice will suck in negativity, attracting lingering illness like cancer, asthma, allergies, tumors, rheumatism and arthritis. No healing will be possible until the person reverses their tonal pattern."

Keys discovered toning by accident. One day her body became filled with a sound so great that she had to express it. "Each time I toned, my body felt exhilarated, alive as it had never felt before, a feeling of wholeness and extreme well-being."

SHOUT OUT!!!
MUSIC CAN ENERGIZE!

A shout is an expression of energy which creates more energy. God is the Author of the "SHOUT OUT!" Music can be an energizing force.

1 O clap your hands, all ye people; shout unto God with the voice of triumph.

2 For the LORD most high is terrible; he is a great King over all the earth.

3 He shall subdue the people under us, and the nations under our feet.

5 God is gone up with a shout, the LORD with the sound of a trumpet.

6 Sing praises to God, sing praises: sing praises unto our King, sing praises.
   Psalm 47: 1,2,3,5,6

> *"I can tell more of what a man is thinking by listening to him play than by hearing him talk..."*
>
> –Papa Jo Jones

THE POWER OF VOICE

Words! There is tremendous power in the human voice! Let me illustrate:

Fabien Maman took healthy blood cells and played a xylophone to them. He photographed the changes in the electromagnetic fields around the cells using Kirlian photography. Subjected to a chromatic scale of frequencies, the slight difference of a half tone would produce a completely different shape and color in the energy field of the cell.

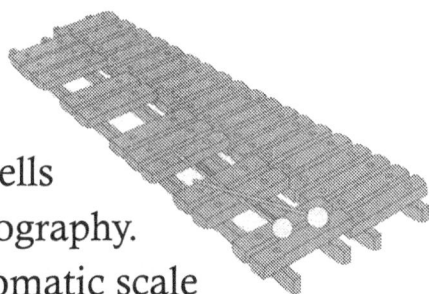

He found that the note 'C' made them longer, 'D' produced a variety of colors, 'E' made them spherical and 'A' (440Hz) changed the color of their energy field from red to pink. In his next experiment, Fabien took a sample of blood from a person's finger. He then asked the person to sing the seven notes of the major scale to their own blood cell. With each note, the cell's energy field changed its shape and color.

When the person sang an 'F' to their own blood cells, the cells resonated perfectly with the voice, producing a balanced, round shape and vibrant colors of magenta and turquoise. He says, "The cells are completely bathed in light and alive with full resonance, clear evidence that this 'F' is the fundamental sound of the singer. Fundamental sound can be very helpful for the physical body through its harmonizing and regenerating effect at the cellular level." From his experiments, Fabien concluded that, "In the human voice there is an added element which cannot be found in any other instrument. The human voice carries its own spiritual resonance. This difference, evident from the photographs, is what makes the voice the most powerful healing instrument particularly when the person needing the healing produced the sounds with his or her own voice."

SOUND FAX

Jim Oliver says that the body responds to sounds that we cannot hear.

He says, "We put the selected sounds exclusively into a pair of headphones and put them on a client's ankles. They responded to the sound even though their ears could not hear the sound. Once you vibrate a part of the body, the blood cells carry this resonance to the whole body very quickly."

CHANT!

Now let's take a look of the concept of chant. Many people seem to avoid the study of chanting because they consider it as "new age." I am not promoting any particular religion when I address the topic of chant; I am simply teaching a concept.

The word chant is defined as a song, hymn, tune, or mantra. The concept of chant is not inherently evil; it's how you use it that determines whether it is good or evil.

I want to particularly focus on what is historically known as the Gregorian Chant. The history of Gregorian Chant begins before the birth of Christ. Chant is based upon the songs sung in the synagogues and Middle Eastern countries. It's fascinating to know that some of today's chants are based upon the actual songs which Jesus sang when he was living in Jerusalem.

Gregorian Chant was adopted by the Christian Church in about the 6th Century and it quickly became an essential part of Christian worship. It was named after Pope Gregory the Great who unified all the chants into one collection. This soon became an essential part of monastic worship and monks would write new chants and take them from monastery to monastery. Eventually there was sufficient Gregorian Chant for all the services – approximately nine a day, seven days a week and even more on great feast days. In the early days, the chant wasn't copied into books. It had to be memorized and it would take monks many years to learn all the different songs. Eventually they worked out a way to write music down, and words and notes were copied into one large book, which all the choir monks would gather round and sing from.

"It is a rhythmic universe…rhythm is the glue that ties together random or external phenomena outside our direct control. The sea the, the heavens, the wind and the stars dance their own rhythmic dance until eternity."

Gregorian chant is the central tradition of Western plainchant, a form of mono-phonic, unaccompanied sacred song of the Roman Catholic Church. Gregorian chant developed mainly in the Frankish lands of western and central Europe during the 9th and 10th centuries, with later additions and redactions. Although popular legend credits Pope Gregory the Great with inventing Gregorian chant, scholars believe that it arose from a later Carolingian synthesis of Roman and Gallican chant. Gregorian melodies are transcribed using neumes, an early form of musical notation from which the modern five-line staff developed during the 16th century.

Gregorian chant was traditionally sung by choirs of men and boys in churches, or by women and men of religious orders in their chapels. It is the music of the Roman Rite, performed in the Mass and the monastic Office. Gregorian chant supplanted or marginalized the other indigenous plain-chant traditions of the Christian West to become the official music of the Roman Catholic liturgy. Although Gregorian chant is no longer obligatory, the Roman Catholic Church still officially considers it the music most suitable for worship.

During the 20th century, Gregorian chant underwent a musicological and popular resurgence.

From Wikipedia, the free encyclopedia

No human culture has ever existed without music.

Dr Tomatis discovered the power of chant after visiting a monastery in France. The new abbot had stopped the monks chanting. The Benedictine monks normally chant for six to eight hours a day. The abbot believed that the Gregorian chant served no useful purpose and that without it they could recapture that time for other things.

The monks had been chanting in order to 'charge up' themselves, but they hadn't realized what they were doing. As the days passed they became more and more tired. A procession of doctors came to the monastery over a period of several months. They changed the monks' diet and sleep patterns but the monks became more tired than ever.

When the abbot called in Dr. Tomatis in February 1967, Tomatis found 70 out of the 90 monks 'slumping in their cells like wet dishrags.' He reintroduced their chanting immediately. By November, almost all of them had gone back to their normal activities, their prayer, their few hours of sleep, and their arduous work schedule.

SOUND FAX

A Merry heart does good like a medicine, and music (or sounds) that you love makes your heart merry!

PRINCIPLES OF
SOUND HEALING!!!

...play skilfully with a loud noise....

What a concept! Play skillfully with a loud noise. Sounds like God likes loud music. WOW! Now lets talk about the principles of sound healing.

Our atoms, molecules, cells, glands and organs all have a vibrational frequency. Sounds from outside our body will stimulate sympathetic vibration in the molecules and cells of our body. The principle of entrainment explains how sound healing works. A harmonious sound projected at a person who is in a state of disharmony will eventually bring them into resonance with the harmonious sound.

The sound wave created by a person singing or playing an instrument will carry information to the receiver of the sound. We all know that a song can be sung with a loving intention or an aggressive intention. When a mother sings a lullaby to her child, the child feels the love in the mother's voice and is rocked to sleep. At a football match, fans sing aggressive chants directed at the opposing supporters and their team. Here the intention is to intimidate.

For me music has always been an effective physician, Healing mind and body!

–Mickey Hart

Dr. Tomatis the French ear, nose and throat specialist has spent over fifty years researching the effects of sound on the human body. Tomatis found that learning difficulties in children are directly related to hearing difficulties. Our hearing range will not only affect our ability to sing in tune but our ability to learn new things and stay healthy. Tomatis proved that our body and brain are literally charged up with energy if we listen to sounds rich in high frequencies. These high frequencies are found in nature in the sounds of the ocean, water flowing and bird songs.

SYMPATHETIC RESONANCE

When two objects have similar vibratory characteristics that allow them to vibrate at the same frequency, they form a resonant system. When a 'C' tuning fork is struck, another 'C' tuning fork close by will also begin to vibrate. For healing to occur there must be a resonance or rapport between healer and patient. (The patient must have ears to hear, i.e. be receptive to the message)

PURE TONE

Jonathan Goldman in his book *Healing Sounds* says, "When we have learned techniques for harmonic toning, the human voice is able to create nearly every frequency, at least within the bandwidth of audible frequency." Goldman offers the simple formula, "If we can find a pure sound frequency coupled with a pure intention, then healing will occur. <u>Pure sound plus Intention equals Healing</u>."

When our body receives a pure tone, our muscles will relax and tension will be released. Pure sound results when the music played is motivated by love and peace. The ambition of the musician should be "world peace."

Dissonant intervals can be used in sound healing to help a person to get in touch with painful emotions. When the dissonance is resolved by sounding the interval above, the person listening will experience a feeling of release, lightness and joy.

After experiencing sound healing through music, most people report a feeling of deep relaxation and an improvement in the function of mind and body. Structural imbalances in the body will often correct themselves during the sound treatment.

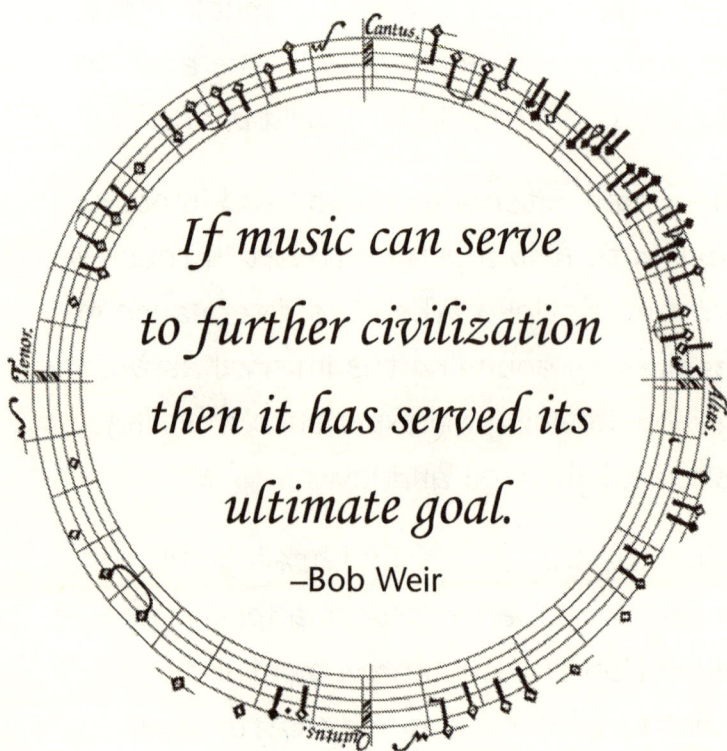

If music can serve
to further civilization
then it has served its
ultimate goal.

–Bob Weir

Music and
THE SPIRIT WORLD

Love and music are the
two wings of the soul.

–Hector Berlioz

Remember that Satan was a musician that fell because of his pride. He will try to use the same trick on you and destroy you with your own talent. I am not talking about religion, but I am talking about love. GOD IS LOVE. Always let love control your music and your musical career. Don't be a hater, be a love motivator!

REACHING YOUR **FULL** POTENTIAL!

HOW TO BE AN ANOINTED MUSICIAN

The anointing is God's Spirit upon a person doing what that person alone could not do. No matter how good you are as a musician or singer you are limited without the anointing. The anointing makes you unlimited! Music is a special energy – it is of this world, but it also acts as a bridge to the spirit world.

I remember an experience in Alaska that changed my thinking about God and the creative power of the anointing. While attending a meeting, the minister called me up to play the drums. I ended up doing a drum solo that lasted over an hour under the anointing. The solo was far beyond anything I had ever done in the clubs, making tremendous power available for the minister to minister that night.

Frankly I did things on that little drum set that I did not know I could do. Why? It was the anointing. I was ministering in music under an anointing and I learned something tremendous. The amazing thing is that the room was packed and remained packed through out the entire solo. Not one person moved. I got so into it that a lady brought me a glass of water while I was doing the solo, because I was sweating so much.

"I have always loved music... we must teach it in our schools; a schoolmaster must have skill in music. Neither should we ordain young men as preachers unless they have been well exercised in music!"

–Martin Luther

2 Samuel 6

1 Again, David gathered together all the chosen men of Israel, thirty thousand.

2 And David arose, and went with all the people that were with him from Baale of Judah, to bring up from thence the ark of God, whose name is called by the name of the LORD of hosts that dwelleth between the cherubims.

3 And they set the ark of God upon a new cart, and brought it out of the house of Abinadab that was in Gibeah: and Uzzah and Ahio, the sons of Abinadab, drave the new cart.

4 And they brought it out of the house of Abinadab which was at Gibeah, accompanying the ark of God: and Ahio went before the ark.

5 **And David and all the house of Israel played before the LORD on all manner of instruments made of fir wood, even on harps, and on psalteries, and on timbrels, and on cornets, and on cymbals.**

THREE THINGS YOU MUST UNDERSTAND TO BE A SUCCESSFUL MUSICIAN

A successful musician is one who finds and develops the potential God has put in him. Always remember your musical talent is a gift from God, a seed. It is up to you to develop, protect and nurture it.

Here are three things that you must understand before developing the potential of your gift:

1. Your mental attitude is the foundation for success or failure.

You must get your attitude right. Humility is the attitude....

...to be made new in the attitude of your minds;

Ephesians 4: 23 NIV

2. Develop your full potential

Develop = to cause to grow, to build and expand, to make stronger and more effective

Potential = that which is possible or can become a reality; the maximum or limit

3. Overcome fear and draw it out.

What people need is on the inside of you. The music to change the world is in your inner man, or your spirit.

"One of the greatest discoveries a man makes, one of his great surprises, is to find he can do what he was afraid he couldn't do."

–Henry Ford

Do you **FEAR** failure

more than you **EXPECT**

success?

Do you **DOUBT** your

true potential?

Would you like to **break** the

chains holding you back from

living your dreams?

Do what

you are afraid

you can't do...

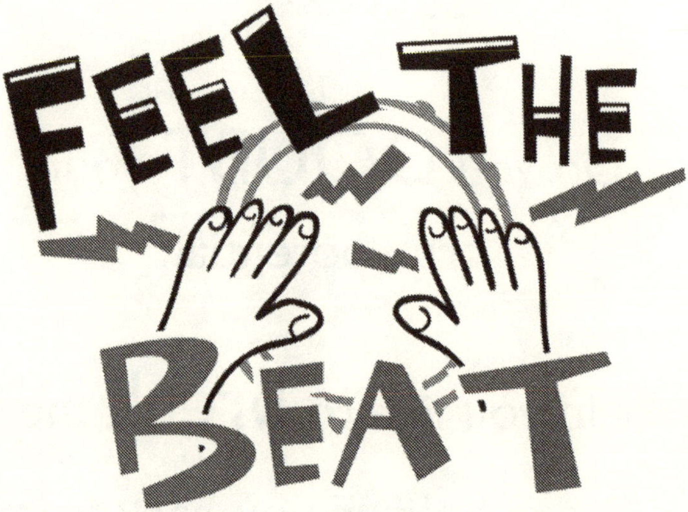
FEEL THE
BEAT

The Creative Artist

The vast potentialities of the creative ability of God within us have never been developed.

There are three major characteristics of the creative artist. They are:

1. Avoids close-mindedness
2. Desires to live an uncommon life
3. Sees the invisible

The artist is a different kind of creature because he/she tends to be more creative than the average person. Most artists are more creative because they are typically more right brain. The right brain is the more creative, visionary side of the mind.

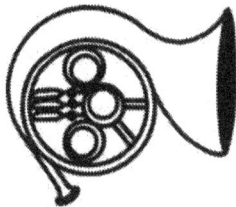

There is nothing better than music as a means for the upliftment of the soul.

–Inayat Khan

Release Your Artistic Creativity

Creativity!

K-E-Y-S

TO

Artistic Creativity

There Is No Problem You Cannot Solve with Creativity!

Creative: original, imaginative, inspired, artistic, resourceful, ingenious, inventive, resourceful, innovative, productive, vision.

Antonym; unimaginative

Creativity is making something out of potential.

Your musical talent is a seed. Seeds have growth potential! Creativity comes out of the human spirit.

Capabilities of the human spirit:

- Gives Guidance
- Solves problems
- Creative energy

Creativity means

bringing forth new things that cause positive change...

"The new thing triggers human experience and understanding."

YOU ARE A CREATIVE BEING.

Humans are a naturally creative species. In Science, politics, business, technology or arts – we depend upon creativity.

Symbols are an example of creativity. They carry deeper, richer meaning.

✦

The cross is an example of a symbol that communicates a deeper meaning of love's sacrifice!

CREATIVE ARTS
AFFECT ON THE QUALITY OF LIFE
Art is based in creativity.

Artists communicate to us about our world. In empirical knowledge we call it the Humanities. This study is basically a look into the artistic ability of man.

Art...
1. Art triggers emotional responses/understanding
2. Art communicates meaning
3. Art is symbolic (parables) of a deeper meaning

Plays, paintings, concerts, social occasions˘

Entertainment is
A R T !

Entertainment defined; a pleasant time, escape from everyday cares.

Entertainment is good! Laughter caused by comedy releases endorphins – chemicals produced by the brain to strengthen the immune system.

MUSIC and DANCE ARE GREAT FORMS OF ENTERTAINMENT!

"ZOE ART"

How Art Works!

Art gives form to (transmit) feelings, reveals spiritual truths, and inspires intellectual development. Art makes us more human and Divine.

Art consists of architecture, paintings, sculpture, theatre, drama, music, dance, literature, and philosophy.

Art leaves room for the imagination.

The point of the spire on the Cathedral = releasing of earthly space to heavenly.

ZOE ART

ZOE is a Greek word that means a new kind of life or the God kind of life. Greek Theatre started out as a spiritual revelation. It was a vehicle for community expression of religious beliefs through employing music, dance and drama.

"It's time to create art that convinces people that this is about real life because it has all the shadows and complexity of real life—light and darkness, certainty and uncertainty, joy and sorrow, humor and seriousness. This is a calling of any Christian artist."

—Kate Bowman

Steps to Unleashing Your ZOE Potential

Decide what you want –
Specific decisions clears your mind and activates creativity

Concentration –
Whatever you concentrate on grows in your life.

Super conscious activity –
Visualization (hold the thought in your conscious mind)

Journaling! –
Write out what you see in your mind and spirit.

Beautiful music takes us
away on a dream . . .
Music expresses the
deepest thoughts of life.

–Arthur Schopenauer

You are creative!

Say this daily:

I AM A CREATIVE BEING!

CREATIVITY IS MY NATURE!

CREATIVITY IS ME!

Thank You for Letting Me Be Mice-elf agin...

God has made you an original...be your creative self...To release more creativity you must understand the three levels of thinking. They are:

1) **Conscious level** – objective analytical

2) **The Sub-Conscious level** (the storehouse of memory)

3) **The Super-Conscious mind** – the source of all creativity, breakthroughs, insights, intuition, inspiration, and imagination. What science calls the super-conscious mind is really the spirit of man.

There are two types of thinking that every artist should understand. The first is **Mechanical Thinking**, black and white, dogmatic thinking, inflexible, often pessimistic. I call it psycho-sclerosis; "a hardening of the attitudes."

The second is **Adaptive Thinking** - open, imaginative, creative, Suspending JUDGEMENT, YES THINKING!!!!

Which type of thinking do you think births more creativity? You got it, adaptive thinking. All creative people have adaptive thinking.

Finally, let's take a look at how the mind works:

Visual – pictures, written words

Auditory- hearing, discussing

Kinesthetic Thinkers – attuned to feelings, emotions.

To release your artistic creativity you must understand what kind of thinker you tend to be so that you can channel your mental energy.

Art is ... a reflection of a greater divine creation. There really is no separation.

–Sufjan Stevens

Human beings were charged by God with a mandate to cultivate the whole earth—which, of course, leads to culture. Humans can't not be cultural; we are, by nature, participants in the world which is our home—warts and all. By the same token, particular industries that designate themselves as religious do not have a lock on the truth. Christians are beginning to recognize—and many artists intuitively realize—that sequestering oneself with only like-minded believers eliminates the possibility of God's revelation in the general culture. Additionally, this means that "Christian music" need not be limited to songs that explicitly mention God or make overtly evangelistic appeals.

–Kate Bowman

CALLING ALL ARTISTS!!!

4 STEPS TO GOD

1. God Loves You!

The Bible says, "God so loved the world that He gave His one and only Son, that whoever believes in Him shall not perish, but shall have eternal life"

The problem is that...

2. All of us have done, said or thought things that are wrong.

This is called sin, and our sins have separated us from God.

The Bible says "All have sinned and fall short of the glory of God." God is perfect and holy, and our sins separate us from God forever. The Bible says "The wages of sin is death."

The good news is that, about 2,000 years ago...

3. God sent His only Son Jesus Christ to die for our sins.

Jesus is the Son of God. He lived a sinless life and then died on the cross to pay the penalty for our sins. "God demonstrates His own love for us in that while we were yet sinners Christ died for us."

Jesus rose from the dead and now He lives in heaven with God His Father. He offers us the gift of eternal life — of living forever with Him in heaven if we accept Him as our Lord and Savior. Jesus said "I am the way, the truth, and the life. No one comes to the Father except by Me." God reaches out in love to you and wants you to be His child. "As many as received Him, to them He gave the right to become children of God, even to those who believe on His name." You can choose to ask Jesus Christ to forgive your sins and come in to your life as your Lord and Savior.

4. If you want to accept Christ, you can ask Him to be your Savior and Lord by praying a prayer like this:

"Lord Jesus, I believe you are the Son of God. Thank you for dying on the cross for my sins. I believe that you died for my sins and that God raised you from the dead. Please forgive my sins and give me the gift of eternal life. I ask you in to my life and heart to be my Lord and Savior. I want to serve you always."

Did you pray this prayer??? Bravo!

I want to send you some free information. Please Email me at Bernard@thesoulofanartist.com

DO IT NOW!!!!

You are now a child of the Living God, the only True God. Welcome to the Family!

reference: www.globalmediaoutreach.com

THE BEGINNING!

Now that you have reached the beginning I will give you my final thoughts.

Discipline is the key to being a complete artist who lives a balanced life. One of the greatest ways to develop discipline is to read a Proverb a day, or one chapter of the biblical book of proverbs each day. Remember Solomon was the wisest man to ever live and he was also the son of an outstanding artist named David. By the way, Solomon was also the richest man who ever lived.

So if you want to be happy, successful and RICH! Read a chapter of proverbs a day. Here is a tip: there are 31 chapters in Proverbs and 30 or 31 days each month. Read the Chapter number that corresponds with the day of the month; example, on the first of the month read Proverbs chapter one and so forth. If you need help give me a shout at Bernard@thesoulofanartist.com

Wisdom for 2day's ARTIST...

Know also that wisdom is sweet to your soul; if you find it, there is a future hope for you, and your hope will not be cut off.

Proverbs 24: 14, The Bible

Psalm 150 (King James Version)

1 Praise ye the LORD. Praise God in his sanctuary: praise him in the firmament of his power.

2 Praise him for his mighty acts: praise him according to his excellent greatness.

3 Praise him with the sound of the trumpet: praise him with the psaltery and harp.

4 Praise him with the tumbrel and dance: praise him with stringed instruments and organs.

5 Praise him upon the loud cymbals: praise him upon the high sounding cymbals.

6 Let every thing that hath breath praise the LORD. Praise ye the LORD.

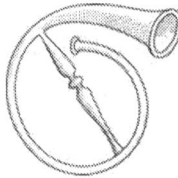

References:
The Holy Bible
Wikipedia, The Free Encyclopedia
Encyclopedia Of Music, Wade Matthews & Thompson
The Healing Power Of Sound - By Simon Heather
Http://Continuingeducation.Suite101.Com/Article.Cfm/Leftbra inrightbrain
http://trust.rdricketts.com/aprayer.html

Who is Bernard Smalls?

I am a creative communicator, an artist, a drummer. As a professional drummer I have played everything from Country to Gospel.

I have studied music at Laney Jr. College, (Oakland, CA.) Behavioral Sciences at National Louis University, Business at American Continental University, Corporate training at The Ken Blanchard Companies, and even Theology at Charismatic Bible College of Alaska and Christian Leadership University of New York.

My passion is music! My God is LOVE. My mission is to bring positive social change to humanity and to help you live the dream that God has placed in your heart as an artist!

*"Your **musical talent** is a **gift** from **God**, a seed. It is up to **you** to **develop**, **protect** and **nurture** it."*
–Bernard Smalls

www.ingramcontent.com/pod-product-compliance
Lightning Source LLC
LaVergne TN
LVHW011403080426
835511LV00005B/400